Laying Nana Down

Poems of Caregiving and Loss

Torie Cooper

Blue Wattle Press

Cover Photograph: © Sydney Holaren

Copyright © 2017 Torie Cooper
All rights reserved
ISBN: 0-9990856-1-1
ISBN-13: 978-0-9990856-1-5

For my Family

and

For all the Caregivers
who have walked
a loved one Home

This collection of poems arose from my experiences in Australia as the sole caregiver for my beloved grandmother who had end-stage colorectal cancer. Nothing in my life had truly prepared me for the emotional and physical challenges of being a full-time caregiver nor was my grandmother prepared for her complete loss of independence. We took the unknown journey together, side by side until she passed away at age 95. This small book of poetry is about caregiving, loss, and love.

Acknowledgements

I would like to thank my family and friends both in Australia and the United States for their encouragement and support in the compilation of this book. Heartfelt appreciation goes to the wonderful staff and volunteers at Calvary Healthcare, Sydney who cared for my grandmother during her countless in-patient admissions and the final hours of her life. In particular, I would like to thank social worker Kathleen Hossack who recognized the value of poetry in providing insight into families and caregivers of long term palliative care patients.

Table of Contents

Acknowledgements	vii
HOME	15
Changing Places	17
Surrender	18
Dignity	19
At-The-Ready	20
One Day	21
The Phoenix	22
Toolbox	23
Out of Petrol	24
Best Self	25
Overboard	26
Alone	27
Caregiver's Jungle	28
Safety Net	29
Stringed	30
Another World	31
Evening Call	32

Kookaburra's Serenade 33

HOSPITAL 35

Relatable 37

Hall of Mirrors 38

Face of Pain 39

Guilt 40

Awaiting Our Turn 41

Overheard 42

Do Not Enter 44

The Wait 45

Showdown 46

Illusion 47

Daydream 48

Overcome 49

River of Tears 50

Room 30 West (For Uncle Terry) 52

FINAL MOMENTS 53

54 Hours 55

Vigil 56

Side by Side	57
Lunar Visitation	58
Fading	59
The Procession	60
Final Moments	61
Metamorphosis	62
Clean	63
Leaving Nana Behind	64

AFTERMATH   65

Heaviness	67
Lesser Things	68
Constant Companion	69
Leftovers	70
Smoke	72
Looking for Work	73
Sorting Life	74
Solar Eclipse	75
Walkabout	76
Flashbacks	77

Caregiving Critique	78
Table of Memories	79
Grief Starts Early	80
Watchful Presence	81
Afterward	83
Notes	84
About the Author	85

"It was the best of times,
it was the worst of times . . . "

Charles Dickens, *A Tale of Two Cities*

Home

Changing Places

Holding Nana's
frail hand
within my own,
feeling paper-thin skin
slide across bony fingers;
remembering
my own hand as a child
being swallowed
by hers.

She was strong years ago
caring for me,
protecting my innocence
and vulnerability.

Changing my nappies,
I now change hers.
Cutting my food
into small chewable pieces,
I now cut hers.
Helping me into
soft flannel pajamas,
I now help her
into nightgown, bed socks.

Roles reversed,
love
remains unchanged.

Surrender

My Grandmother
drops a green pill
onto the floor
unable to reach it.

Telephone rings,
neighbour knocks
loudly on front door,
tomato soup boils over
sides of small saucepan.

Standing dead-tired
middle of the floor,
I burst into tears
not knowing
what to do first.
Utterly overwhelmed,
stressed, alone,
I silently beg for help.

Dignity

Slowly position
my grandmother
safely
upon cold toilet seat,
gently wiping her
when she finishes.
Fresh clean undergarments
replacing soiled ones,
clothes changed
as needed.

Struggling to maintain
her dignity
under enormously
undignified
circumstances.
Old age, frailty,
colorectal cancer
strip away decorum.

Only love
softens such indignities,
restores respect,
soothes the frustration
of dependency.

At-The-Ready

On high alert
throughout
long chilly night.
No quality rest,
no deep sleep
despite longing to
drown within it.

Listening for sounds
of breathing,
sounds of need:
a fall to the ground,
bedside bell ringing,
soft cry for help.

Hyper-vigilant,
listening to analog clock
mark precious seconds;
bone-weary mind, body
ready for anything.

One Day

One day,
I'll eat a hot meal
from start to finish
without interruption
but not today.

One day,
I'll stretch stiff legs
with a long
leisurely walk
but not today.

One day,
I'll meet a friend
for coffee,
catch up on family news
but not today.

One day,
I'll finally finish
neglected book
laying upon the end table
but not today.

The Phoenix

Threw myself
into the fire,
flames consuming
every remnant
of who I once was.

Burned beyond recognition,
rising as a Phoenix
from its own ashes;
initiated as 'Carer.'

Moving through
scorched
uncharted landscape
of pain, nausea, bleeding,
confusion, tears,
incontinence.

Heart smoldering
with trepidation,
loneliness, sorrow;
praying for rain.

Toolbox

Maxalon, Fentanyl,
Hydromorphone,
Lorazepam,
Haloperidol, Lyrica,
Endone, Cyclizine,
Transexamic acid.

White tablets, yellow tablets,
green tablets,
transdermal patches,
powders, creams, syringes;
tools of the
Palliative care trade.

Weapons of choice
against pain, nausea,
bleeding, anxiety;
a caregiver's toolbox,
heavy
with responsibility.

Out of Petrol

Working on empty,
out of fuel.
Batteries dead,
no more energy.
But somehow still pushing
reaching deep within,
holding onto
an unseen anchor.

Cannot,
must not
stop
otherwise
I may not restart.

Nana must be fed,
medicated,
clothes changed,
bottom wiped,
helped into bed.

Many needs
require many tasks.
I am one
working as many,
working on empty.

Best Self

One day I'll consider
these difficult times
as some of my finest.
I'll realize
challenged by
sorrow and hardship,
standing upon
wearied legs,
I have never been
so strong,
so courageous.
One day
I'll look back
and see
my best self.

Overboard

Drowning in a sea
of endless tasks,
desperate for a life-ring.
Exhausted,
I hold my grandmother
above water
while my own head
goes under,
struggling for air.
I must not
allow us both to submerge.
Learning to tread water
in stormy seas is perilous.

Alone

Bright red blood
drips rapidly
onto bathroom's
black and white tiles,
rolls down Nana's
thin brittle legs
staining pale blue socks,
pink satin slippers.

Grab thick pads,
pressing firmly against
angry tumour.
Notice
mucous and feces
smeared across
toilet seat,
lower portion
of blue nightgown.

Odour sickening,
cannot surrender myself
to thoughts of vomiting.
Must step up
take control,
must handle this;
no-one else is coming.

Caregiver's Jungle

Dense wilderness of medicine,
equipment,
incontinence aids,
tasks to complete,
symptoms to monitor.

Vines threaten
to trip me, strangle me,
no machete
to thin them out.
No compass
to guide me
to familiar and safe territory.

Calvary Hospital calls
asking
how I'm doing?
I'm lost in the jungle.

Safety Net

They come,
hearing my heart's silent cries.
They phone,
interrupting my self-neglect.
They listen,
hearing what remains unspoken.
They support,
holding my crumbling self.
Calvary Hospital
ID cards
clipped to their shirts,
hanging from lanyards;
wingless angels
caring for me.

Stringed

Endlessly performing,
I have become
a marionette
moved by an unseen
puppeteer;
invisible strings
lifting my weary body
onto life's darker stage.

Dancing awkwardly
with the sick and dying,
knowing how the play ends
but unsure
of how it will unfold.
Waiting
for the final
curtain call.

Another World

Unremitting stress
befriends
unending fatigue.
Can't think straight,
completely overwhelmed.
Outsiders see with
different eyes,
speak a language
I no longer understand.
I live on Mars,
barely remembering Earth.
Survival,
day to day.

Evening Call

Bedside bell rings,
intruding upon
restless dreams.
Staggering
down dark hallway
2:30 am.
Cold, bone-weary,
thinking through
semi-dry concrete,
mentally preparing for
every possibility.

What need
might be addressed
this time?
Toilet? Bleeding? Nausea?
Pain? Fever? Confusion?

Tiny elderly woman
buried beneath layers
of thick warm blankets
blinks beneath
bright ceiling light,
softly apologizing
for waking me.
Touched by her frailty,
love overpowers
my weariness.

Kookaburra's Serenade

Cold dark morning,
dawn barely blushing
upon distant horizon.
Kookaburra sings
as blanketed gurney
cradling
Nana's pint-sized form
is gently lifted
into the ambulance.
She will never
return home.

Sitting upon
mottled grey branch
in nearby gum tree,
kookaburra's voice
is crystal clear,
each distinct note
full of meaning
like a bugle
playing Last Post.

Ambulance carrying
precious family matriarch
quietly drives away
down sleepy
tree-lined avenue.

Kookaburra continues
his soulful serenade
as I watch the vehicle's
bright interior lights
grow smaller, disappearing.

One true blue Aussie
acknowledging another;
Nana must have liked that.

Hospital

Relatable

Passing fellow visitors,
exchanging
subdued smiles,
a knowing nod.
Weary faces,
a mirror image
of my own.
Head down
in the elevator
staring at my shoes;
I need to clean them.

Hall of Mirrors

I see them, hear them
everywhere.
Red-eyed, wet cheeked,
quivering lips,
sobs that
tear the heart
from its anchorage
of normality.

Within the halls,
dining rooms,
elevators . . .
sights and sounds
of sorrow
that will one day
be mine.

Face of Pain

Slowly wandering quiet halls
stretching stiff legs,
taking a break.
Rounding a corner,
tall young man
leans heavily
against cream-colored wall,
hands rammed deeply
into pant pockets,
staring straight ahead.

Facial muscles taut
with emotional strain
following
loved one's passing,
tears threatening
to spill over tired
red-rimmed eyes.

Gently squeezing his arm
I hear my voice quietly say,
"I'm so sorry for your loss."

I walk away.
Too late to construct
a protective wall
around my psyche, my heart;
the young man's
pained expression
of utter anguish
forever imprinted
upon my memory.

Guilt

Boy in elevator
cradled within his father's
strong arms,
inconsolable.
'Poppy' passed away,
probably the boy's
first encounter
with life's final mystery.

One hour later,
my 95-year-old grandmother
is discharged.
She is going home.
Guilt unexpectedly
surrounds me.
Why is *my* family so lucky?

I wish there were
a back door leading out
of Calvary Hospital,
one I could smuggle
my grandmother through
out of sight
of other families,
younger patients.
Cannot relax
until we are in the taxi.

Awaiting Our Turn

Families take turns
rolling the dice,
waiting for
'concealment' trolley
covered with clean
white cloth.

Quietly,
it wheels
down long hall
passing
most patient's rooms
but always
entering one of them;
a strange game
of roulette.

Tomorrow,
trolley may silently,
stealthily stroll
the halls again,
this time
parking alongside
your beloved's bed.

Overheard

Thin blue curtains
separating patients
in shared rooms
shield the eyes,
not the ears.

Delicate conversation
always begins
the same way:
"I'm worried about
your liver"
(or kidneys or colon).
The voice is kind,
the message devastating.
Nothing more
can medically be done;
return tickets sold out.

Surrendering to fate,
facing a firing squad
of toxins,
failing organs,
patient bravely asks
about the time
remaining.
Greater courage
awaits the answer,
"Long days to short weeks."

Heavy silence follows
before soft tearful voice
begins to speak
of loved ones,

other concerns.

An arrow,
straight and true
pierces my heart,
cannot be pulled out.

Time to walk
the halls again.
Stunned, saddened,
terrified
by the powerful reminder
of my own mortality.

Do Not Enter

Walking past private room
with the
'Do Not Enter' sign;
door ajar,
blue curtain drawn.

Hearing sturdy zipper
of body bag
securing
someone's beloved;
wincing
at the sound.

Sorrow for a face
never to feel
sunlight or rain,
never again
to cry or laugh.

Perhaps,
a lingering farewell kiss
still warm
upon lifeless cheeks;
a face sealed
in someone's heart
for eternity.

The Wait

Bedside vigil,
next room down.
Hour after hour,
day after day.

Darkened room,
shadowed figures
stand, pace, sit,
softly speaking,
. . . waiting.

Showdown

The good guys
become the enemy
wearing black hats,
pushing
nursing home care.

Nana,
small and frail,
cannot defend herself,
needs me to be strong,
fulfil her one final wish.

What will happen?
What can be done?
I stand terrified,
hand trembling
above my revolver,
staring down
dusty main street
at High Noon
looking into the eyes
of doctors, social worker,
pastoral care.

I am outnumbered.
They stagger their shots,
striking me
with bullets
designed not to harm
but to help.
I lay bleeding
upon the ground
watching
tumbleweeds pass;
poised to surrender.

Illusion

New patient
settles into private room,
cool clean sheets
against thin bare legs.
Head turned toward
large sunny window,
familiarizing herself
with the
expansive view.

She does not know
another patient's
precious final breath
was taken in that very bed
only a few hours ago.

Does not know
his belongings were placed
inside a pink plastic bag,
slippers removed
from the floor.
Does not know
how many tears
were shed.

There is no trace
of the deceased,
nothing left behind
only the illusion
of newness,
the secret kept intact;
she is lying upon
a revolving death bed.

Daydream

Botany Bay,
deep blue and glistening
viewed from
second floor window.
Sea crashes hard,
exploding white, foamy
onto jagged rocks.

Across the shore
large passenger planes
roar down long runway
of Kingsford-Smith
International Airport
lifting skyward
towards
midday sun,
banking northeast.

For a moment,
I hear coyotes yipping
in the Sonoran Desert
beneath
bright summer moon,
calling me
back to Arizona.

Behind me,
four seriously ill
women
lie upon their beds;
magpies chase
the coyotes away.

Overcome

Stepping aside,
leaning back
against pale wall,
allowing passage
of long
narrow trolley.

I know what lies
beneath
the clean white sheet
but not *who*.

Upon whose face
would my eyes rest
if the sheet
were removed
and the body bag
unzipped?
A mother? Father?
Sister? Uncle?
Grandparent?

Someone
who has ripped the fabric
of another's heart
passes
within inches of me;
my mind drowns
with the enormity of it.

River of Tears

Second floor, South wing.
Walk carefully past
quiet private rooms:
Slippery When Wet.

Tears spill beneath
drawn blue curtains
soaking
carpeted hallways,
forming rivers of tears;
grief in motion.

Slowly flowing
onto mirrored elevators
going Down,
always Down,
transporting sinking,
drowning hearts.

Seeping
onto Ground Floor
past the gym,
outpatient services,
vending machines.
Large crucifix
hanging upon the wall
watches;
Christ weeping.

Liquid sorrow
gently opens sliding
Front Entrance doors,
tenderly rolling

down smooth concrete steps
beneath a different sky.

Heartbreak finds its way
into parked cars,
buses, trains, and planes;
leaving a winding
trail of tears
behind.

Room 30 West (For Uncle Terry)

The bed in room 30 West
lies empty.
Shaving razor
in the bathroom gone,
cupboards and drawers cleared,
chairs pushed back
against the walls,
curtains open.

How many patients
enter this room alive
but leave breath-less?
What were their names?
Is there any minute
trace of them left
after the floor is polished
and bed sheets changed?
Are the tears of their loved ones
stored somewhere unseen?

The bed in room 30 West
lies empty;
a portal to another world,
silently waiting
for the next traveler.

Final Moments

54 Hours

My grandmother took
54 hours to die
following
95 years of living;
inner youth versus old bones,
cancer.

No IV fluids, oxygen,
food or water;
nothing life-saving
entering tiny frail body
only opioids, anti-seizure,
anti-anxiety meds,
. . . and love.

Her ancient body
fought death
like a full-grown marlin
hooked by
an experienced fisherman,
straining against
line, rod, and boat,
succumbing
to eventual, inevitable
fatigue;
reeled in
by a Greater Force.

My grandmother took
54 hours to die
following
95 years of living.

Vigil

Long quiet vigil,
darkened hallways,
nurses speaking in whispers.

Hour after hour,
heavily-laden
with fatigue, sorrow,
we watch your body
grow weary.
Waiting, ever waiting
for the final exhale.

Waiting for your tiny
exhausted body
to rest.
Waiting for your gentle soul
to fly home.

Side by Side

Lying beside you
upon narrow bed,
wondering if this will be
our final night together.

Your frail,
battle-weary body
struggles to continue living,
back of throat
gurgling slightly.

My arm,
lightly draped over
your small thin frame
feels the rising,
falling of your chest.
I listen,
not knowing when
your last earthly breath
will be.

Sorrowful, exhausted,
longing for deep sleep
yet not wanting to miss
'the end,'
I cannot afford to doze off.

Yet I do;
awoken
by a kind nurse
covering me
with soft blue blanket.
My worn face
quickly looks up into yours,
relieved you are still here.

Lunar Visitation

Moon peeks through
hospitals' large windows,
watching us
watching you.

Like a comforting friend
moon lends
its silent presence,
reminding us of vastness,
time's endless cycles,
mysteries beyond
human comprehension.

Moon maintains vigil
from afar
until earth-spin and orbit
temporarily separate us
from view.

Perhaps,
this is moon's message
to those of us who
watch and wait;
your passing
will simply be
a temporary separation
from view.

Fading

Autumn leaves slowly fade
replacing
the green of their prime
with the reds,
yellows, oranges
of their passing;
falling to another world.

So, my grandmother
also changes,
slowly fades,
withering into a fragile leaf
awaiting the next breeze
to lift her
from life's branch.

The Procession

Word spread throughout
hospitals' second floor
like wildfire
on a hot windy day:
Joyce Hicks was finally dying.

She had far surpassed
every educated,
experienced prediction.
But now
the time was at hand,
no more practice drills.

And so, they came,
staff and volunteers
saying their goodbyes
to the tiny woman
with the
thousand-mile stare.

Holding her limp hand,
whispering in her ear,
massaging her feet,
reciting the rosary;
small acts of kindness
filling the room
with love.

Final Moments

I hold the soft warm hand
I may not hold tomorrow,
eyes resting upon familiar
much loved face.

Softly whispering,
'I love you Nana'
into ears with
diminishing
ability to hear.

Tenderly kissing soft
sweet-smelling cheeks,
I remember my
child-self doing the same.

How precious
are these final moments
watching my grandmother
grow wings and fly?

Metamorphosis

My grandmother
lays within a chrysalis
of warm blue blankets,
slowly transforming.

Earth-bound
caterpillar-body of cancer
shifting, changing,
moving.

Imperceptibly,
moment by moment
invisible
moist wings unfurl,
dry, stretch,
awaken to flight.

A quiet exhale,
. . . she is free.

Clean

Washed at birth,
washed at death.
Transitions
are messy,
full of where
one has been.

Leaving Nana Behind

Cold early hours
of Spring's first morning.
Exhausted,
mournful yet relieved
at suffering ended,
we slowly walk
hospital's long muted halls,
past sleeping patients'
darkened rooms
towards large lobby,
main front doors.

We carry bags
containing Nana's clothes,
reading glasses,
hearing aid, hairbrush.
She no longer needs them.

We have always left
hospital
with my grandmother,
now we are leaving
without her;
entrusting her body
to others.

Silently melting
into taxi's back seat
lost in thought,
heading home through
drowsy deserted streets,
we begin writing
a new chapter of our lives;
not knowing how to form
the first sentence.

Aftermath

Heaviness

A loved one passes
and our hearts sink,
along with the setting sun
beneath
a great dark shadow.

Lesser Things

I've cried more
for lesser things;
broken objects,
failed interviews,
small disappointments.

But this loss
is *enormous*.
My beloved grandmother -
mentor, confidant,
best friend
vanished from my eyes,
my touch, my ears
forever.

Internal ocean
of tears dry,
not one drop remaining.
Stunned,
looking out across
the desiccated,
lifeless seabed of my soul;
feeling nothing,
feeling everything.

Constant Companion

Grief is my cumbrous
constant companion;
unseen, silent.

Sleeping
beside me at night,
intruding
upon restless dreams.

Walking beside me
in daylight,
accompanying me
to supermarket,
post office, bank.

A fellow passenger
on bus, train, ferry.
Standing beside me
while I wipe dishes.

Leftovers

Threw away leftover
baby wipes, latex gloves,
cream for nappy rash,
bed sores;
things no longer needed.
Neighbour receiving
your unopened bag
of disposable
undergarments.

Collected
surplus medications
into large plastic bag,
carrying them
to Chemist
for proper disposal.

Removed your name tag
from small red walker
that steadied
increasingly thin
weak legs.

Called Occupational Therapy
to collect it
along with
other loaned items:
bed rail, toilet-raiser,
wheelchair,
anti-bedsore mattress.

Carefully
cleaning them,

I recall once thinking
I'd be glad to see
the last of these items
some day.

Now,
warm uncontrollable tears
roll down my cheeks,
drip off my chin.

It's difficult to release
these final remnants
of our time together;
these no-longer-needed
objects that
tell the story
of our journey.

Smoke

Loved one on fire,
light grey smoke
billowing
rapidly
out of tall concrete tower
into cool morning air.
Woronora Cemetery & Crematorium
doing the unthinkable
on our behalf.

Looking for Work

Suddenly unemployed,
out of a job.
No longer
full-time Carer
now you're gone.

Free time on my hands,
what should I do with it
aside from missing you?

Hard to stop
being a caregiver;
cannot find switch
turning off autopilot.

Everywhere,
eyes search for
an elderly person
who needs me.

Resist temptation
to ask strangers
if they require assistance.
Can I trim their nails?
Wash their hair?
Take them to the toilet?

Your small
vulnerable body is gone,
I miss not caring for it.

Sorting Life

Watch my sister
newly flown from America
sort our grandmother's clothes,
folding them with care,
categorizing them:
Donate, Discard, Keep.

Can barely observe
let alone participate
in this heart-wrenching
process.

Easily visualizing
Nana wearing
each item my sister holds.
Remembering myself
dressing her
as though
it were yesterday;
feeling her small
shrinking body
swallowed within
slacks, shirt, cardigan,
nightgown, dressing gown.

Tears cannot be contained
behind eye's
weakened walls,
cheeks wet with grief.

"Let's take a break,"
my sister kindly suggests.
We walk together in sunshine,
carrying the heaviness
of inner rain.

Solar Eclipse

She was like the sun,
always there;
every sunrise, every sunset
of my life.

Bright, warm,
life-affirming;
a permanent fixture
in my sky.

Now,
I walk beneath
clouds of mourning,
too light-less
to cast a shadow,
missing sweet sunshine.

Walkabout

My grandmother's spirit
gone walkabout
across this vast continent
she loved.

Above shimmering
deep blue sea, sandy beaches,
thick green forests
of eucalypts.

Over lanolin infused
backs of merino sheep,
waving fields of wheat,
mobs of kangaroo.

Down quiet streets
lined with
flowering jacarandas,
over Outback's red heart.

Skimming Sydney's
'Coat-Hanger,'
white-sailed Opera House,
bobbing ferries.

Drifting through
the old Strand Arcade,
Darrell Lea's,
Victoria's Basement.

My grandmother's spirit
gone walkabout
across this vast continent
she loved.

Flashbacks

Memories of your passing
stalk me
like a wild thing
in dense dark jungle.

I cannot un-see
that which was seen,
cannot un-hear
that which was heard,
cannot un-feel
that which was felt.

Weary moon
apologetically peers
through small window,
bathing my wide-eyed,
sleepless face
in soft light;
we both remember.

Caregiving Critique

Sometimes,
during evening's
lengthy silence
I second-guess myself;
decisions I made,
things I did or did not do,
words I spoke or did not say.

Wishing I had been
stronger, more aware
as your caregiver Nana.
My best,
when you needed me most,
a watered-down version
of who I presently am.

Everything is clearer
now I'm rested,
better fed.
I'm more insightful,
a better problem-solver;
20-20 vision
once all is said and done.

Yet those
hardships, trials,
inexperience, shortcomings
became the bedrock
upon which I have grown.

I know
you understand Nana.
Now I must release myself
from occasional 'if only.'

Table of Memories

Surrender myself
to tearful tsunami
as two men carry
your round kitchen table
to the back of
St. Vincent de Paul truck.

Decades of memories
stuck like glue
to smooth wooden surface;
cannot scrape them off.

Heartfelt chats
over steaming cups of tea,
meat pie and sausage roll lunches,
endless games of cards.

Humble table adorned
with colorful flowers,
small bottomless bowl of candy,
plastic lace tablecloth.

Powerful gathering place
for family, friends,
laughter and tears;
your loving presence
always central.

Grief is a heavy blanket
covering everything:
a loved one,
their clothes,
treasured knick-knacks,
favorite foods,
kitchen table.

Grief Starts Early

Grief begins
while the one we love
is still among us.
Heaviness increasing
as we watch
muscles, bones, organs
slowly weaken, fail.
Body passing
when it can do no more.

Hearts, minds
saturated
in fathomless sadness
born of love,
swallowed by
surging seas of sorrow.

Tears slowly dry
with the seasons,
easing sharp sense
of loss,
converting heartbreak
into purpose;
living for two.

Watchful Presence

Not gone,
only unseen.
Watching over us,
loving us
as she always did.

A gentle angel
whose tender presence
remains with us
through our long days
and longer nights.

Comforting us
through sadness,
smiling with us in joy;
a perpetual loving companion.

Our forever Mother,
Grandmother,
Great-Grandmother,
and Friend.

Afterward

Thank you for reading this small book of poetry. If you're a caregiver, I hope these poems led you to discover you are not alone in walking a loved one Home. There are many of us. If you aren't a caregiver, I hope this book provided a glimpse into the day to day life of one. Caring for a loved one with a serious or terminal illness is a labour of love that takes an enormous emotional and physical toll. The experience is profound and changes each caregiver in a unique manner. It takes time for caregivers to heal in the aftermath of a loved ones' passing but in the end, we learn that we are stronger than we knew. The simplicities of daily life become far more precious thanks to our experiences walking a loved one Home.

Notes

a. Colorectal cancer (my grandmother's illness) is a 'messy' cancer and difficult to manage. Please take the time to see your doctor regularly for an examination and colonoscopy. Don't allow fear or inconvenience to prevent you from saving your own life.

b. Most communities offer a range of services to help you care for a loved one. Doctors, social workers, and community nurses can help you get started.

c. For those grieving a loved one, bereavement counselling is offered in many communities, hospitals, and churches. Speaking with an objective listener such as a trained counsellor can be help you adjust to new circumstances and challenges.

About the Author

Torie Cooper is an Australian-American poet who makes her home on both sides of the Pacific. For over a year she was the sole caregiver for her much-loved grandmother who had terminal colorectal cancer. Torie is the author of the book *Nature: A Collection of Poems.* Her poetry has appeared in the journals, *The Avocet* and *The Stray Branch.* This is her second book of poetry. Currently, Torie is working on a small book for caregivers that is part memoir and full of practical tips.

www.ingramcontent.com/pod-product-compliance
Lightning Source LLC
Chambersburg PA
CBHW032207040426
42449CB00005B/482